The Hungry Fox

a Fable Told in Rhyme

Once upon a time, in a magnificent forest deep,
Winter held sway, and food was scarce and cheap.
Snow and ice patches lay thick on the ground,
Yet the joy of the season was all around.

The forest stretched as far as the eye could see,
Beneath a sky as blue as it could be.
Its many residents, when speaking, loved to rhyme,
A charming tradition, practiced all the time.

Our tale begins with a lonely red fox,
Emerging from his den beneath the rocks.
You see, Fox had just awakened from his slumber,
Cold, drowsy, and with hunger that made him lumber.

The cold had made his body stiff as wood,
So he stretched his limbs as far as he could.
Where should he begin his search for food?
He pondered, surveying the neighborhood.

After all, how hard could it really be?
That's the adventure we're about to see.

The fox's journey begins
Right here
The Monkey
Page 14
The Bear
Page 6
The Rabbits
Page 10

The Elephant
Page 18
The Giraffe
Page 22
The Raccoon
Page 26
The Squirrel
Page 30
The Owl
Page 34

The Fox and The Bear

At the river's edge, on the verge of the forest, stood a bear who had just finished fishing for his lunch. A pile of fresh fish lay on the ground, and the bear hummed a happy tune while the fox drooled with desire.

The singing bear noticed his guest's presence and waved for him to approach. "Greetings, my friend! Help yourself and have no fear. This bear has lots of fish to spare," he called out.

The fox stepped forward, eyes wide and mouth watering. He pulled with his paw one fish, then two, then three... and continued until he had amassed a big pile of food by his side.

Seeing this, the bear's smile turned into a frown. He stepped between the greedy fox and the stack of fish and said, "Had you not been so blinded by greed, you would've had half of my meal, little fox. But I do not share with greedy folks."

Ashamed of his actions, the hungry fox watched as the bear devoured the fish one by one, then slunk away, leaving the place in regret.

The Fox and The Rabbits

While wandering through the woods, the fox overheard a joyous chant. Hoping for a better chance to satisfy his hunger, he picked up the pace and headed toward the sound. Upon arrival, he found a colony of fluffy rabbits digging up vegetables while performing a happy dance.

"Hop, top... Hop and prance!" the rabbits cheerfully sang in a circle, holding hands. The ongoing ceremonial harvest left the fox in a trance.

"Hello, big, strong mister fox. Would you help us harvest our carrots?" asked one rabbit in the middle of his hops.

The fox looked at the dirt-covered rabbits and replied, "I'd rather not sweat and dirty myself for some measly carrot tops."

The rabbits, astonished by the fox's response, interrupted their chants and hurried to cultivate their carrots. "Had you not been so arrogant, you would have enjoyed this marvelous vegetable. But we do not help those who don't help a friend," they said at the end of their chant.

When the fox saw the big, juicy carrots leave the ground, his mouth watered and his eyes widened. This time, he had only his pride to blame.

The rabbits tossed their harvested treasure into a bag and dragged it away, hopping and prancing all the while, very satisfied. Meanwhile, the fox, tortured by his hunger and regret, nearly cried.

The Fox and The Monkey

Long hours had passed, and the fox had found nothing to eat. As he walked, a banana suddenly landed right before his feet. Although he had never tasted one before, he had heard it was soft and sweet.

Neat! I found myself a nice little treat! thought the fox as he reached for the fallen fruit. But before he could peel and eat his treat, a crackling sound above his head made his heart skip a beat. It was a swift monkey swinging on the tree branches, who then took a seat on the largest one.

The fox quickly hid the banana between his tail and his feet.

"Good day, Mister Fox," said the brown monkey politely. "It seems I've dropped my meal. Have you seen a fruit with a yellow peel?"

"No, I haven't seen your meal," muttered the hungry fox, trying to stay still.

"Aha! And what is that you're trying to conceal behind your heel if it isn't my meal?"

The fox, at a loss for words, stood there immobile, fighting the urge to squeal.

The monkey came down from the tree and took back the banana poorly hidden between the fox's feet.

"Had you not lied to me, I would have gladly shared my meal with you." Said the monkey. "But I cannot forgive those who try to steal."

Once again, the fox, very ashamed of his actions, watched the monkey disappear.

The Fox and The Elephant

Later that day, the sun was bright, and the fox hadn't yet found a single bite. That's when he stumbled upon a baby elephant down the hill, next to a huge tank of milk that he was rocking back and forth, about to spill.

The fox looked at the silky white milk, and malice twinkled in his eyes. Although the elephant was a baby, he was many times larger than the fox. But the fox thought he could easily outsmart the youngster with cunning and lies. The milk, obviously, would be his prize.

"Say, kid, I bet you can't scratch your head with your foot," said the fox, taking the youngster by surprise.

"I can too," replied the baby elephant, who was not yet wise.

"Let's make a deal. If you fail, I'll take half of your milk, and if you win, you can make me do anything you want."

The baby elephant tried but failed and ended up on his flank, and the fox, feeling astute, quickly jumped on the milk tank. But something held him back: it was the baby elephant's mother's long, strong trunk.

"Shame on you, devious fox. Trying to trick my baby out of his milk," said the mother before swinging the fox by his tail and sending him flying through the air.

The Fox and The Giraffe

The fox was walking away from his last encounter when he heard a loud, cracking crunch. He looked in the sound's direction and saw a giraffe stretching her long neck while feeding on a tall tree's branch.

Munch... Munch... Munch..., continued the giraffe with her crunch, apparently unconcerned with the presence of the newcomer or the big pile of plump and juicy mushrooms lying beneath her in a bunch.

The starving fox seized the moment to guzzle down a few pieces of the rare treat. But the mushrooms, although succulent, caused him dizziness and a stomach ache. Not long after, he started to lament.

The giraffe, seeing the moaning fox, leaned towards him and whispered, “Had you not jumped on these mushrooms without asking, I would have warned you they cause terrible aching. But no worries, it’ll pass in minutes, if I’m not mistaken.”

And fortunately, it did. The fox recovered from that terrible affliction and vowed never to eat anything again without permission.

The Fox and The Raccoon

The constant feeling of hunger put the fox in quite a grumpy mood, and his stomach kept growling as he roamed the neighborhood. It had been a long time since he had started his search for food. Suddenly, he stopped as he thought he heard his name echoing in the woods.

"Hey, Mister Fox!" the voice kept calling, getting nearer and clearer.

The shouting voice belonged to a fuzzy-looking raccoon who ran towards the fox and stood on a tree log just two feet away from him.

The fox, whose only interest was food, gave the empty-handed raccoon a disinterested look and said, “Beat it, little dude”.

“No need to be rude! I’m not looking for a feud,” replied the snubbed raccoon whose intentions were genuinely good.

“I would if I could. But all I can think about is food.”

The offended raccoon stepped back and said:

"Had you not been so rude, I would have had shown you the path to some campers' leftover food."

The fox quickly regretted his insolence, but by the time he looked back, the raccoon has already disappeared. And once more, the fox was left thinking he wasn't indeed very shrewd.

The Fox and The Squirrel

Not very far from there and after a while, the fox noticed some tree branches shaking and nuts bouncing on the ground, forming an abundant pile. He approached the tree and saw a squirrel climbing up and down its trunk while flashing a big, wild smile.

“Hey there, neighbor. Can I trouble you for a favor?” shouted the agitated squirrel without interrupting his labor.

The fox followed the energetic tiny creature
with his eyes then nodded in agreement.

“I need to do a chore. Can I trust you to guard
my treasure of nuts, if it’s no bore?”

The fox thought the nuts must burst with flavor,
so he cunningly agreed to do this favor.

“I will be back long before night!” shouted the
squirrel, already out of sight.

Immediately, the fox sat next to the supply of nuts and sneakily consumed one nut once in a while, until he finished almost a quarter of the pile. A moment later, the squirrel came back as he had promised. And with just a glance, he noticed that many nuts were missing from his harvest.

“Oh no... I was planning to give you a big bag of nuts had you not broken your promise. Shame on you for not being honest,” said the very displeased squirrel.

The fox imagined the big full bag and quickly regretted his little snack. Once more, he would have to go back empty-handed, and still starving, to his shack.

The Fox and The Owl

That night, the fox returned to his cozy den, his stomach still growling but his mind full of the day's lessons. He decided to rest and continue his search for food tomorrow. Just as he settled down, something caught his eye: a majestic owl hovering above him, clutching a large bag filled with all the foods he had missed during his wanderings.

"Good evening," greeted the owl, her wings spread wide.

"Hi," replied the fox with a weary sigh.

"I didn't mean to pry, but I've been watching you from the sky."

"Why?" asked the fox, feeling a bit shy.

"I saw you were struggling, but you couldn't help being sly."

The fox, now deeply ashamed, hung his head.

"Don't worry, little friend," said the owl, gently gliding down. "I brought you a feast. But promise me you'll change your ways, or at least you'll try."

The fox, eyes wide with gratitude, nodded earnestly.

"Here, take it all," offered the owl, placing the bag of goodies on the ground.

"No, I'll just take what I need," said the fox, shaking his head.

"I see you've learned your lesson about greed. Greed is not a kind deed."

"No, it isn't indeed," agreed the fox. "But what about my slyness?"

"Before you act, think about the consequences," advised the owl.

"You're right... And what about my pride?"

"Sometimes, pride should be put aside."

"What if I can't help being rude?" asked the fox.

"That's no excuse to not be good," replied the owl.

"And what about stealing?"

"You must fight that urge with all your might."

"How can I earn trust?"

"Always ask for permission and never break your promises. Trust is a must."

"Thank you, wise owl," said the fox, smiling genuinely.

"You're welcome, dear friend," said the owl, taking to the sky. "Remember, change starts with trying."

And as the owl flew away, they both called out, "Goodbye."

The fox pounced on the bag of goods and ate with delight,
For his hunger had been such a mighty plight.
Never before had he seen such a wonderful sight.

Once full, he stretched, readying for sleep,
Counting his lessons instead of sheep.
The snow felt warm, so he sank in deep.

This is bliss, he thought with a yawn,
His hunger now completely gone.
And right before he drifted to sleep,
He made a promise, just before dawn:

I'll cherish the Owl's wise advice,
Shake off my vices, and always be nice.
For I've learned that everything comes with a price.

Follow us on Instagram on @little.reader.shop

The Hungry Fox Tales series includes:

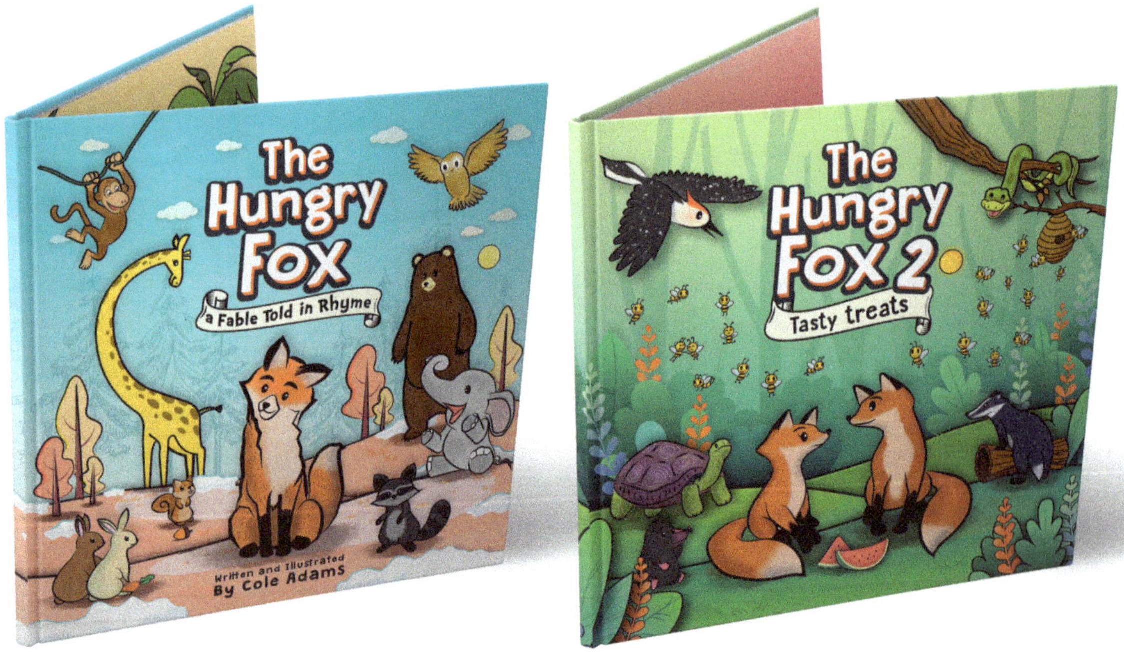

Also available in French, Spanish, and Italian.

Milton Keynes UK
Ingram Content Group UK Ltd.
UKHW051656020624
443369UK00005B/19

9 798869 380937